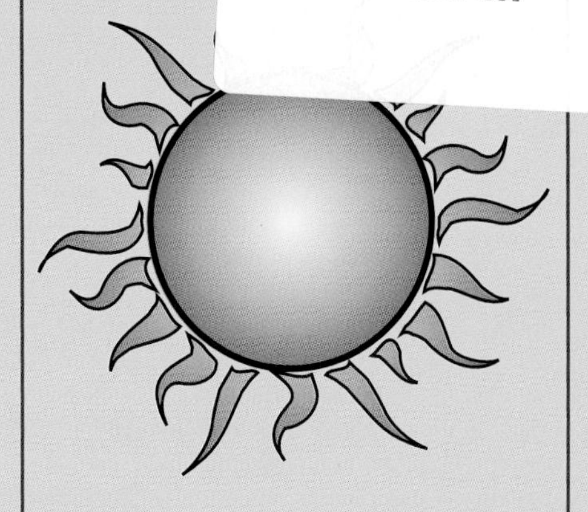

LEO

23 July – 22 August

Abbeydale Press

Leo is the fifth Sun Sign . . .

1. Aries, The Ram: 21 March–19 April
2. Taurus, The Bull: 20 April–20 May
3. Gemini, The Twins: 21 May–20 June
4. Cancer, The Crab: 21 June–22 July
5. Leo, The Lion: 23 July–22 August
6. Virgo, The Virgin: 23 August–22 September
7. Libra, The Scales: 23 September–22 October
8. Scorpio, The Scorpion: 23 October–21 November
9. Sagittarius, The Archer: 22 November–21 December
10. Capricorn, The Goat: 22 December–19 January
11. Aquarius, The Water Carrier: 20 January–18 February
12. Pisces, The Fishes: 19 February–20 March

Published by Abbeydale Press
An imprint of Bookmart Limited. Registered Number 2372865.
Trading as Bookmart Limited, Desford Road,
Enderby, Leicester LE9 5AD, UK.

ISBN 1-86147-0363

Produced for Bookmart by Scribble Ink,
4 The Old Maltings, Hopton, Suffolk IP22 2QZ, UK.
Telephone: 01953 681564. Fax: 01953 681574.
Printed in Singapore.

The word ASTROLOGY comes from two Greek words – ***astron*** (star) and ***logos*** (knowledge). Astrology is based on a belief that there is a definable link between patterns in the heavens and patterns here on Earth. Astrologers use the positions of stars and planets at the time of an individual's birth to predict certain influences that will shape the character and subsequent life of that person. By compiling a detailed birthchart (or horoscope), they then seek to determine positive and negative forces likely to apply to that individual.

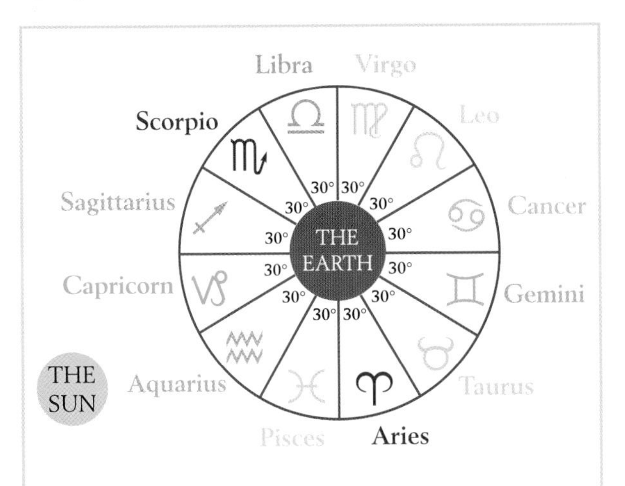

The starting point for astrology is the Zodiac Wheel. The wheel is an imaginary band around Earth, divided into 12 segments of 30°. Each segment is named after a nearby star constellation, and everyone born when the Sun is passing through that segment has the appropriate "Sun Sign".

INTRODUCTION:

DO HOROSCOPES actually work? Many people regard astrology as no more than a bit of harmless fun – but deep inside even the most cynical lurks a primitive suspicion that there may be more to this ancient art than they care to admit.

The birth of astrology is lost in the mists of time. The earliest known horoscopes emerged in Babylonia around 500 BC, and serious study of the stars began with the Greek philosopher Ptolemy's book *Almagest* in the 2nd Century.

Over the years, this work was built upon by many great thinkers, including Abu Ma'shar (Persia), Guido Bonatti and Marsilio Ficino (Italy) and Nicolaus Copernicus (Poland). By the 16th Century the principles of astrology were firmly established and Queen Elizabeth I's court astrologer, John Dee, was a respected figure.

As technology improved, studying the stars split into two disciplines: astronomy and astrology –

the latter dismissed by scientists on the grounds that its conclusions could not be proved.

Scientific or not, astrology continued to fascinate and new knowledge of the heavens was put to good use in developing the detailed theories that underpin modern astrology.

Because everyone born under Leo has a unique birthchart, each will have a different astrological "destiny" in store. For example, a strong physical connection with matters relating to the heart can manifest itself as a strength or a weakness (or neither!), depending on the actual person concerned. And even some of the most general traits associated with Leo may be absent if other, more powerful influences are present in an individual's horoscope.

This pocket guide is designed to summarise the main Leo characteristics and influences. Check them out and decide for yourself if the stars have got it right!

PLANETS

Every Sun Sign is associated with, and ruled by, one or more of the 10 astrological planets, each of which exerts specific influence on the sign(s) it rules – and any birthcharts in which it appears. Leo is ruled by the Sun.

☉ SUN	*The Sun provides the energy at the heart of our solar system. It represents the vital life force within everyone, symbolising authority, pride, strength and courage.*
☽ MOON	*The Moon complements the bold qualities of the Sun, standing for the rhythms of emotional life, nurturing qualities and a person's relationship with their body.*
☿ MERCURY	*Swift-orbiting Mercury represents quick and enquiring thinking, communication and commerce. Also linked with less desirable traits like cunning and crime.*
♀ VENUS	*Venus shares the female circle-and-cross glyph, and is the planet associated with grace, love and beauty. It can also represent vanity and a desire for luxuries.*
♂ MARS	*Blood-red Mars shares the male circle-and-arrow glyph, and represents direct energy and ambition. It suggests positive qualities like heroism, but also selfishness.*
♃ JUPITER	*The largest planet, Jupiter, stands for self-confidence, adventure, exploration and expansion. Jupiter can also influence good athletic ability and risk-taking.*
♄ SATURN	*Once thought to be the outermost planet, Saturn is the planet of order, self-discipline, security and duty. Linked with the skeleton, which gives the body form.*
♅ URANUS	*Uranus – discovered only in 1781 – represents social change, dramatic upheavals and rapid technological advance. A strong influence for all sorts of innovation.*
♆ NEPTUNE	*The secret world of imagination, dreams, spirituality and fantasy is associated with Neptune. Traditionally linked with the sea and its mysterious depths.*
♇ PLUTO	*Late-on-the-scene Pluto represents life's darker forces and is connected to war, pestilence and death. More positively, it influences regeneration after destruction.*

ELEMENTS

The astrological world consists of four basic elements – Fire, Earth, Air and Water. Each exerts its own distinctive influence on a horoscope, and rules three Sun Signs, imparting its elemental character to those signs. Leo is a Fire Sign.

FIRE
Fire crackles and burns like a relentless spirit, providing a symbol for human enthusiasm, energy and drive to achieve.

EARTH
The Earth is the solid core of our being and stands for all that is reliable, unchanging, predictable and material in life.

AIR
Think of a bird soaring free as a metaphor for Air, which thus represents the freedom of ideas, thought, and communication.

WATER
Water finds its own level, often flowing in mysterious ways as an ideal symbol for inner feelings, emotions and the human soul.

QUALITIES

The 12 Sun Signs are divided among three essential qualities – Cardinal, Fixed and Mutable. The Cardinal Quality supports activity and initiative. The Fixed Quality indicates reliability and stability. The Mutable Quality stands for adaptability and change. Leo is a Fixed Sign.

GENDER

Each Sun Sign is either "masculine" or "feminine". This is not a direct link with sexuality, but rather an indication of a general approach to life. The masculine (positive) signs are associated with an outgoing, assertive disposition and the feminine (negative) signs are associated with an intuitive, receptive character. Leo is a masculine sign.

ZODIAC BRIEFING:

SUN SIGN	QUALITY	GLYPH
1. ARIES	Cardinal	♈
2. TAURUS	Fixed	♉
3. GEMINI	Mutable	♊
4. CANCER	Cardinal	♋
5. LEO	Fixed	♌
6. VIRGO	Mutable	♍
7. LIBRA	Cardinal	♎
8. SCORPIO	Fixed	♏
9. SAGITTARIUS	Mutable	♐
10. CAPRICORN	Cardinal	♑
11. AQUARIUS	Fixed	♒
12. PISCES	Mutable	♓

SUMMARY OF INFLUENCES

	ELEMENT	GENDER	RULING PLANET
	Fire	Masculine	Mars
	Earth	Feminine	Venus
	Air	Masculine	Mercury
	Water	Feminine	The Moon
	Fire	Masculine	The Sun
	Earth	Feminine	Mercury
	Air	Masculine	Venus
	Water	Feminine	Mars/Pluto
	Fire	Masculine	Jupiter
	Earth	Feminine	Saturn
	Air	Masculine	Uranus/Saturn
	Water	Feminine	Neptune/Jupiter

LEO:

THE KING of Beasts is proud, loyal and fierce. So are Leos, who like to be at the heart of the action and take charge, along with any responsibility that's going.

There's no doubt about it – Leos take pride in their achievements and perceived status. But their drive is about more than a simple desire to win. Deep down, they're strongly motivated by the need to be seen in a noble light. Although they want to come out on top in life, that hunger for nobility can sometimes be powerful enough to push Leos into courageous or even reckless self-sacrifice.

But despite a larger-than-life embrace of the world's cares, Leos have a need to be loved for themselves rather than their grand actions and energising personalities. And Leos fear they may not be up to the expansive image they create and can undervalue themselves accordingly.

Yet when everything goes well, a Leo can be a

wonderful source of inspiration to family and friends, bringing pleasure and happiness – basking in the appreciation of those who have gravitated into that warm Leo circle. But when things don't go so well, and they feel unappreciated or ignored, Leos can turn quite nasty.

POSITIVE LEONINE QUALITIES

- *Happy disposition and playful sense of fun*
- *Honest and very loyal to family and friends*
- *Generous host who welcomes everyone warmly*
- *Pride in discharging responsibilities effectively*

NEGATIVE LEONINE QUALITIES

- *Tendency to withdraw and sulk when hurt*
- *Weakness for keeping up appearances at all costs*
- *Arrogance, taking credit where it's not due*
- *Occasional indifference to the needs of others*

oooooo LUCKY LINKS oooooo

Colours – Yellow, orange, gold
Gemstones – Crystal, tiger's eye

LEO MAN

If typical, with no forces in his birthchart that outweigh the natural influence of his Sun Sign, the male Leo will show some or all of these key characteristics . . .

- *Lithe and slim – unless lazy and over-indulgent*
- *Has boundless sex appeal in young adulthood*
- *Loves to show off and be the centre of attention*
- *Seems confident and in control at all times*
- *Affectionate, generous, trusting and totally loyal*
- *Needs reassurance he's as good as he pretends*

LEO WOMAN

The typically Leo woman, if ruled by her Sun Sign rather than contradictory influences in her birthchart, will show some or all of these key characteristics . . .

- *Slim and elegant, prone to weight gain when older*
- *Likes a life full of excitement and stimulus*
- *Tends to take the lead in all social situations*
- *Expects loyalty and is deeply hurt by betrayal*
- *Gives full-hearted commitment to loved ones*
- *Wants to be admired, tends to show off subtly*

LEO CHILD

A characteristic young Leo can be very active and constantly at physical rather than mental play – play which may get reckless. An outgoing, happy nature is complemented by a generous disposition. Leos love being the centre of attention but take badly to discipline and restraint.

Attraction of opposites?

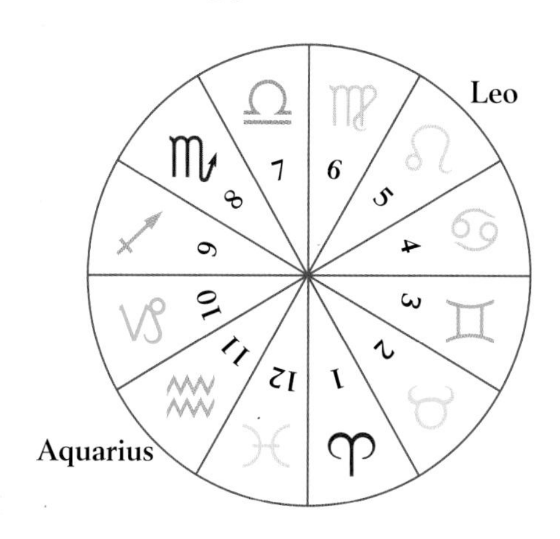

Leos are rarely drawn to members of the opposite and complementary sign – though Aquarians offer Leos ability to step from the limelight and value themselves for what they are.

SUCCESS turns Leos on, so they like their friends and family to be high achievers – but not to the point where that bright Leo sun is actually eclipsed by others.

When it comes to friendship, both male and female Leos are gregarious creatures, always enjoying being with friends. Leos are lively and entertaining in company, though their persistent playfulness and love of boisterous fun can be wearing. Despite genuine Leonine generosity of spirit and deed, Leo friends can be fickle – if they feel people are not responding to their gestures with respect and admiration, Leos can drop them. And those with a competitive streak of their own can soon come into conflict with a larger-than-life Leo friend.

Family life works best if a Leo partner is allowed to believe that they're undisputed top cat – whatever the truth of the matter. If two Leos team up, separation of responsibilities can allow each partner to dominate in one field.

Leos love to entertain lavishly, so the home will often be full of people and always have a lively, happy atmosphere.

Leos like attractive, comfortable homes which buzz with activity. But the habitual open house policy only goes so far. If a Leo feels that family territory is being encroached on in any way, fun and frolics are quickly forgotten and there is no more determined defender of home and family than a Leo.

LEO PARENTS

The parent whose birthchart has a typically Leo pattern, without contradictory influences, will show some or all of these key characteristics when raising children . . .

- *Makes serious effort to raise children really well*
- *Takes tremendous pride in kids' achievements*
- *Tries to teach offspring as much as possible*
- *Warm, generous and giving of time and interest*
- *Protective and supportive of all their children*
- *Puts pressure on children to perform, succeed*

CATS AND BIRDS don't get on well, though every so often newspapers will publish a picture of a canary sitting happily on moggy's head – a good story precisely because it is a perfect example of the unexpected.

So it is with people born under the different signs of the zodiac. It's possible to calculate how well (or badly!) Leos *should* relate to members of every other Sun Sign, and the results are shown opposite.

Generally, signs that share the same element – Fire, Air, Earth or Water – relate harmoniously, as will those sharing one of the three qualities – Cardinal, Fixed or Mutable. When it comes to the ruling planets, however, relationships with members of the opposing sign are usually quite difficult – so Leos should beware of Aquarians bearing gifts!

But remember, there will always be those striking attractions of opposites that prove the rule.

Leo Relationship Chart

The chart shows how well a typical Leo relates to those born under all 12 Sun Signs. Check to see if your own personal relationships show a Leonine compatibility pattern . . .

Rating =	Easy	Hard	Stressful
ARIES	✔		
TAURUS		?	
GEMINI	✔		
CANCER	✔		
LEO	✔		
VIRGO	✔		
LIBRA	✔		
SCORPIO		?	
SAGITTARIUS	✔		
CAPRICORN			✘
AQUARIUS		?	
PISCES			✘

LOVE comes easily to Leos. Leo men act like a magnet to the opposite sex, especially in their prime, and Leo women have natural beauty and *joie de vivre* that most men find irresistible. And Leos have an abundance of love to give.

Typical young adult Leos tend to fall in and out of relationships quite frequently. Their romantic expectations are high – sometimes *too* high – and it can take time and experience before they manage to identify the sort of partner with whom they wish to spend the rest of their lives.

A Leo's lover must be adoring, never putting them in the shade. They must be desirable and admired by others and like being spoiled by an attentive Leo who will shower affection and gifts. They must both want and need their Leo lover, yet never become over-dependent or clingy. For Leos, love must be *very* special.

When things go well, Leo in love is romantic, attentive, caring and loyal – drawing patent

strength and happiness from the relationship. Sex will be boisterous and fulfilling. But if a Leonine relationship starts to fail, Leo pride may become problematical. The rejected Leo may find it hard to let go of his or her cherished mate, yet become deliberately inattentive. If the Leo is a victim of infidelity, the deep wound thus caused will take a long time to heal and may be masked by cruel indifference.

LEO LOVERS

Where a strong Leonine influence dominates the birthchart, a Leo lover will show all or some of these characteristics . . .

- *Totally committed to the chosen partner for life*
- *Likes giving – and receiving – generous gifts*
- *Expects to be adored and respected by partner*
- *Needs partner to be dependent on their strength*
- *Glows with sheer happiness at being in love*
- *Willingness to make any sacrifice for love*
- *Desire for partner to be seen and envied by others*
- *Feeling the relationship is very special indeed*
- *Capable of aggressively defending a partner*

LEOS are always happiest in the company of people they love, because the heart is strongly linked with Leo.

Typical Leos are bouncy, energetic and healthy people – with one proviso. They need to be loved, and if feeling unappreciated or deprived of affection will start to complain or develop all sorts of niggly minor complaints.

Leos can become involved in intense activities that are pursued forcefully, but every so often they become exhausted and need to rest and recharge the batteries. This should not be taken as a sign of weakness or impending illness.

Leonine patients are difficult, appreciating a short period of sickness when everyone is fussing over them, but soon becoming fretful and wanting to "get up and go", even if that is not possible.

Fevers or illnesses that seem to spring from nowhere are typically Leonine ailments. Heart

and circulatory problems may develop and Leos often suffer from back problems. The wrist and ankle joints can give trouble, often as a result of an accident. Like all those born under a fire sign, Leos tend to be accident-prone.

Strengths & Weaknesses

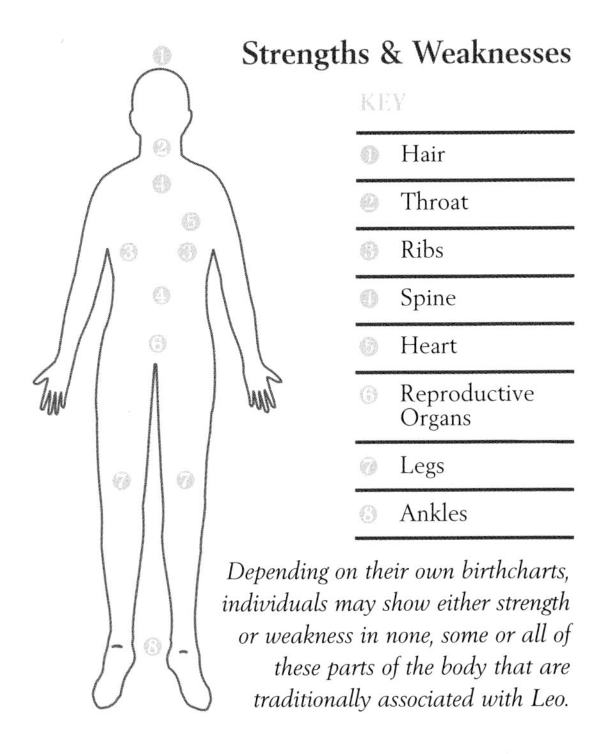

Depending on their own birthcharts, individuals may show either strength or weakness in none, some or all of these parts of the body that are traditionally associated with Leo.

A LEO will rarely give anything but a truly excellent impression at that first interview, but beware. Leos are adept at putting themselves in the best possible light and are not above over-stating their qualifications and achievements. But they're usually underestimating their true worth anyway, so this tendency to exaggerate may not be a problem. Leos are good workers who can be at their very best under pressure.

Typical jobs are in fields like sales and marketing, financial services, PR, promotion, management, performance arts, the law. . . anywhere that allows full expression to the relentless Leo compulsion to take the lead and become the centre of attention (and win the plaudits). If they can't meet this need in the marketplace, Leos often become self-employed.

As a boss, Leo man or woman is a hugely self-confident leader who inspires subordinates, but can soon struggle if authority is undermined. The Leo boss is very generous with rewards for

effort, but hates failure and may take the full credit for any achievements.

As a worker, the Leo man or woman needs to be respected, whatever the job – and will soon quit if feeling undervalued. If that trap is avoided – as it easily can be simply by lavishing praise – Leos are loyal, hard-working employees who can and do motivate those around them.

LEO LEISURE

Where primary Leo influence predominates in a birthchart, the "lion" at play will show all or some of these characteristics . . .

- *May be into keep fit to maintain physical shape*
- *Has strong desire to excel even in leisure time*
- *Enjoys all competitive sports and pastimes*
- *Loves it when friends can admire performance*
- *Can be interested in theatre or showmanship*
- *Penchant for any activities that bring pleasure*
- *Takes real delight in family-orientated leisure*
- *Often eats out and goes to clubs or parties*
- *May take leisure activities to damaging excess*

A–Z KEYWORDS

ASCENDANT (or RISING SIGN) – the point on the eastern horizon of a zodiac birthchart.
ASPECT – the angle in degrees between planets in a birthchart.
ASTROLOGY – the study of relationships (or "coincidences" in modern parlance) between actual events and planetary positions at the time.
BIRTHCHART (or HOROSCOPE) – chart that calculates the positions of Sun, Moon and planets at the time and place of an individual's birth, representing a combination unique to that person.
CELESTIAL SPHERE – that view of the heavens seen from Earth, as though Earth were the centre of the Universe.
CONJUNCTION – term used when two or more planets are positioned close together in a birthchart.
CUSP – point at which two houses of a birthchart adjoin, often allowing influences associated with another Sun Sign to impact on an individual's horoscope.
DESCENDANT (or FALLING SIGN) – the point on the western horizon of a zodiac birthchart.
ELEMENT – the four elements of Fire, Air, Earth and Water are linked with general characteristics that apply to related zodiac signs.
FORECAST – Attempt to predict the future based on previous planetary patterns and their known future positions.
GENDER – the 12 Sun Signs are equally divided between the "masculine" and "feminine" genders, symbolising aspects generally associated with the male and female character respectively.
GLYPH – symbol representing Sun Sign, planet etc.
PLANET – eight major bodies excluding Earth that move around the Sun. The Sun and Moon are included to make 10 "astrological" planets. Each planet "governs" one or more Sun Signs, imparting its own characteristics.
QUALITY – the 12 Sun Signs are equally divided between three essential qualities, Cardinal, Fixed and Mutable, each with distinct impact on the relevant signs.
SUN SIGN – that sign of the zodiac occupied by the Sun on an individual's date of birth (often incorrectly termed "star sign").
ZODIAC – imaginary spectrum that divides the solar system into 12 segments, each named after a constellation of stars close by.
ZODIAC SIGNS – the 12 segments of the zodiac, numbered in an anticlockwise direction, based on their positions at the spring equinox.